D0114525

The Prayers That Avail Much
Journal

The Prayers That Avail Much
Journal

by
Word Ministries

Harrison House
Tulsa, Oklahoma

Unless otherwise indicated, all Scripture quotations are taken from the *King James Version* of the Bible.

The Prayers That Avail Much Journal
ISBN 0-89274-831-1
Copyright © 1995 by Word Ministries, Inc.
38 Sloan Street
Roswell, Georgia 30075

Published by Harrison House, Inc.
P. O. Box 35035
Tulsa, Oklahoma 74153

Presented to

_____

By

_____

Date

_____

Occasion

_____

Introduction

The earnest (heartfelt, continued) prayer of a righteous man makes tremendous power available [dynamic in its working] (James 5:16 AMP).

Prayer is fellowshipping with the Father — a vital, personal contact with the God Who is more than enough. We are to be in constant communion with Him.

Prayer is not to be a religious form with no power. It is to be effective and accurate and bring *results*.

Prayer that brings results must be based on God's Word. That Word does not return to Him void — without producing any effect, useless — but it *shall* accomplish that which He pleases and purposes, and it shall prosper in the thing for which He sent it. (Isa. 55:11.)

God did *not* leave us without His thoughts and His ways for we have His Word — His bond. God instructs us to call Him, and He will answer and show us great and mighty things. (Jer. 33:3.) God moves as we pray in faith — believing. He tells us to come boldly to the throne of grace and *obtain* mercy and find grace to help in time of need — appropriate and well-timed help. (Heb. 4:16.)

Prayer must be the foundation of every Christian endeavor.

Our Father has not left us helpless. Not only has He given us His Word, but also He has given us the Holy Spirit to help our infirmities when we know not how to pray as we ought. (Rom. 8:26).

We pray to the Father, in the name of Jesus, through the Holy Spirit according to the Word!

The power lies within God's Word. It is anointed by the Holy Spirit. The Spirit of God does not lead us apart from the Word for the Word is of the Spirit of God. We apply that Word personally to ourselves and to others — not adding to or taking from it — in the name of Jesus. We apply the Word to the *now* — to those things, circumstances, and situations facing each of us now.

Prayer does not cause faith to work, but faith causes prayer to work.

When we use God's Word in prayer, this is not something we just rush through uttering once, and we are finished. Do *not* be mistaken. There is nothing "magical" nor "manipulative" about it — no set pattern or device in order to satisfy what we want or think out of our flesh. Instead we are holding God's Word before Him. We confess what He says belongs to us.

We expect His divine intervention while we choose not to look at those things that are seen but at the things that are unseen for the things that are seen are subject to change. (2 Cor. 4:18 paraphrase.)

Prayer based upon the Word rises above the senses, contacts the Author of the Word and sets His spiritual laws into motion. It is not just saying prayers that gets the results, but it is spending time with the Father, learning His wisdom, drawing on His strength, being filled with His quietness, and basking in His love that bring results to our prayers.

— Word Ministries, Inc.

▼ ▼ ▼

"Faith changes hope into reality."   ◄

— KENNETH E. HAGIN

_____

_____

_____

_____

_____

_____

_____

_____

_____

_____

_____

_____

_____

_____

_____

_____

_____

_____

_____

_____

_____

_____

_____

_____

Therefore I say unto you, What things soever ye desire, when ye pray, ◄
believe that ye receive them, and ye shall have them.

MARK 11:24

▲ ▲ ▲

▼ ▼ ▼

► *"God's promise is as good as His Presence."*

— ANDREW MURRAY

_____

_____

_____

_____

_____

_____

_____

_____

_____

_____

_____

_____

_____

_____

_____

_____

_____

_____

_____

_____

_____

► *If you remain in me and my words remain in you, then you will ask for anything you wish, and you shall have it.*

JOHN 15:7 *Good News*

▲ ▲ ▲

▼ ▼ ▼

"I can get more out of God by believing Him for one minute than by shouting at Him all night."

— SMITH WIGGLESWORTH

_____

_____

_____

_____

_____

_____

_____

_____

_____

_____

_____

_____

_____

_____

_____

_____

_____

_____

_____

_____

_____

_____

_____

So I tell you to believe that you have received the things you ask for in prayer, and God will give them to you.

MARK 11:24 *New Century Version*

▲ ▲ ▲

▼ ▼ ▼

► *"Nobody ever sought God without being heard."*

— LESTER SUMRALL

_____

_____

_____

_____

_____

_____

_____

_____

_____

_____

_____

_____

_____

_____

_____

_____

_____

_____

_____

_____

_____

_____

► *Call unto me, and I will answer thee, and show thee great and mighty things, which thou knowest not.*

JEREMIAH 33:3

▲ ▲ ▲

▼ ▼ ▼

"The main secret of success in the development of the blessing is the ◄
exercise of a humble dependence on the Lord."

— ANDREW MURRAY

_____

_____

_____

_____

_____

_____

_____

_____

_____

_____

_____

_____

_____

_____

_____

_____

_____

_____

_____

_____

_____

_____

Make Yahweh your only joy and he will give you what your heart ◄
desires.

PSALM 37:4 *Jerusalem*

▲ ▲ ▲

▼ ▼ ▼

► *"Faith refuses to see (as reason for doubting) anything contrary to the Word of God."*

— F. F. BOSWORTH

_____

_____

_____

_____

_____

_____

_____

_____

_____

_____

_____

_____

_____

_____

_____

_____

_____

_____

_____

_____

_____

_____

► *And this is the confidence that we have in him, that, if we ask any thing according to his will, he heareth us: and if we know that he hear us, whatsoever we ask, we know that we have the petitions that we desired of him.*

1 JOHN 5:14, 15

▲ ▲ ▲

▼ ▼ ▼

"The first part of prayer is praise, the second is intercession for others, ◄ and the third is petition, when we ask for our needs to be met."

— PAT ROBERTSON

_____

_____

_____

_____

_____

_____

_____

_____

_____

_____

_____

_____

_____

_____

_____

_____

_____

_____

_____

I give praise to God, whose servant I have been, with a heart free from ◄ sin, from the time of my fathers, because in my prayers at all times the thought of you is with me, night and day.

2 TIMOTHY 1:3 *Basic English*

And if we know that he hear us, whatsoever we ask, we know that we have the petitions that we desired of him.

1 JOHN 5:15

▲ ▲ ▲

▼ ▼ ▼

► *"If a thought is held in the heart sincerely, and if that thought goes out toward the living God, it is a prayer."*

— ORAL ROBERTS

_____

_____

_____

_____

_____

_____

_____

_____

_____

_____

_____

_____

_____

_____

_____

_____

_____

_____

_____

_____

_____

► *You know when I sit and when I rise; you perceive my thoughts from afar.*

PSALM 139:2 *New International Version*

▲ ▲ ▲

▼ ▼ ▼

"Prayer is a joy and a privilege, available to all of God's children." ◀

— CORRIE TEN BOOM

_____

_____

_____

_____

_____

_____

_____

_____

_____

_____

_____

_____

_____

_____

_____

_____

_____

_____

_____

_____

_____

_____

_____

You will show me the path of life; in Your presence is fullness of joy; at ◀
Your right hand are pleasures forevermore.

PSALM 16:11 *New King James Version*

▲ ▲ ▲

▼ ▼ ▼

► *"The great Father God is a love God. His very nature — because He is love — compels Him to care for us, protect us, and shield us."*

— KENNETH E. HAGIN

_____

_____

_____

_____

_____

_____

_____

_____

_____

_____

_____

_____

_____

_____

_____

_____

_____

_____

_____

_____

_____

_____

► *But God commendeth his love toward us, in that, while we were yet sinners, Christ died for us.*

ROMANS 5:8

▲ ▲ ▲

▼ ▼ ▼

"Our intercession for all men is not so much for God to extend His ◄
mercy. This He has already done through Jesus. Our intercession is
mainly to break the bondage that the devil has over men."

— WILFORD H. REIDT

_____

_____

_____

_____

_____

_____

_____

_____

_____

_____

_____

_____

_____

_____

_____

_____

_____

_____

_____

I solemnly tell you that whatever you as a Church bind on earth will in ◄
Heaven be held as bound, and whatever you loose on earth will in
Heaven be held to be loosed.

MATTHEW 18:18 *Weymouth*

▲ ▲ ▲

▼ ▼ ▼

► *"Jesus taught His disciples not how to preach, only how to pray."*
— ANDREW MURRAY

_____

_____

_____

_____

_____

_____

_____

_____

_____

_____

_____

_____

_____

_____

_____

_____

_____

_____

_____

_____

_____

► *If you get your life from Me and My Words live in you, ask whatever you want. It will be done for you.*
JOHN 15:7 *New Life Version*

▲ ▲ ▲

▼ ▼ ▼

*"Faith clamps down the teeth of God's Word on the seat of the enemy's ◄
pants and hangs on until Satan quits!"*

— MARILYN HICKEY

Stand firm therefore, having girded your loins with truth.... ◄
EPHESIANS 6:14 *New American Standard*

▲ ▲ ▲

▼ ▼ ▼

► *"You can live in an attitude of prayer constantly, being in communion and fellowship with your heavenly Father every hour of the day."*

— KENNETH COPELAND

_____

_____

_____

_____

_____

_____

_____

_____

_____

_____

_____

_____

_____

_____

_____

_____

_____

_____

_____

_____

_____

► *Be unceasing in prayer.*

1 THESSALONIANS 5:17
Weymouth

▲ ▲ ▲

▼ ▼ ▼

"Determined prayer by faithful prayer warriors can make possible the ◄ successful gospel invasion of the foreign fields."

— GORDON LINDSAY

For, though walking in flesh, we are not warring according to the flesh, ◄ (for the weapons of our warfare are not fleshly, but mighty through God for the casting down of strongholds).

2 CORINTHIANS 10:3, 4 *Worrell*

▲ ▲ ▲

▼ ▼ ▼

► *"Prayer is the place of exchange between you and God. It is where you tell God all that is in your heart, and He puts in you what is in His heart."*

— EDWIN LOUIS COLE

_____

_____

_____

_____

_____

_____

_____

_____

_____

_____

_____

_____

_____

_____

_____

_____

_____

_____

_____

_____

► *Delight yourself in the Lord and he will give you the desires of your heart.*

PSALM 37:4 *New International Version*

▲ ▲ ▲

▼ ▼ ▼

"Prayer is more than 'needs' relying on 'omnipotence,' it is worship." ◀

— ROY HICKS

_____

_____

_____

_____

_____

_____

_____

_____

_____

_____

_____

_____

_____

_____

_____

_____

_____

_____

_____

_____

Let my prayer be like incense placed before you, and my praise like the ◀
evening sacrifice.

PSALM 141:2 *New Century Version*

▲ ▲ ▲

▼ ▼ ▼

► *"The prayer armor is for every believer, every member of the Body of Christ, who will put it on and walk in it."*

— CAROLYN EAST, WORD MINISTRIES

_____

_____

_____

_____

_____

_____

_____

_____

_____

_____

_____

_____

_____

_____

_____

_____

_____

_____

_____

► *But through all, with prayer and supplication, praying at every moment in spirit, and keeping watch in it with steady tenacity: and praying for the holy.*

EPHESIANS 6:18 *Fenton*

▲ ▲ ▲

"If we find that plan of God and work within it, we cannot fail." ◄
— E. STANLEY JONES

For I know the thoughts and plans that I have for you, says the Lord, ◄
thoughts and plans for welfare and peace and not for evil, to give you
hope in your final outcome.

JEREMIAH 29:11 *Amplified*

▼ ▼ ▼

► *"Man was made for God, to seek Him, to find Him, to grow up into His likeness and show forth His glory."*

— ANDREW MURRAY

_____

_____

_____

_____

_____

_____

_____

_____

_____

_____

_____

_____

_____

_____

_____

_____

_____

_____

_____

_____

_____

_____

_____

► *For whom He foreknew, He also predestined to be conformed to the image of His Son, that He might be the firstborn among many brethren.*

ROMANS 8:29 *New King James Version*

▲ ▲ ▲

▼ ▼ ▼

"I come in in the morning and I spend time before we do anything else, ◀
praying, reading the Bible. I encourage all my department heads who
are born again...to do the same. I go from office to office praying in their
rooms and over their typewriters."

— FORMER PRESIDENT RONALD REAGAN

_____

_____

_____

_____

_____

_____

_____

_____

_____

_____

_____

_____

_____

_____

_____

_____

_____

_____

And in the morning, a long time before daylight, he got up and went ◀
out to a quiet place, and there he gave himself up to prayer.

MARK 1:35 *Basic English*

▲ ▲ ▲

▼ ▼ ▼

► *"It is necessary for us to take time to pray. A ruffled lake cannot reflect the stars in the heaven or the sun in the sky. And a disturbed and restless soul can get very little vision of God."*

— HENRIETTA C. MEARS

_____

_____

_____

_____

_____

_____

_____

_____

_____

_____

_____

_____

_____

_____

_____

_____

_____

_____

_____

► *Be careful for nothing; but in every thing by prayer and supplication with thanksgiving let your requests be made known unto God. And the peace of God, which passeth all understanding, shall keep your hearts and minds through Christ Jesus.*

PHILIPPIANS 4:6, 7

▲ ▲ ▲

▼ ▼ ▼

"Give your all to Him, and He will give His all to you." ◄
— AIMEE SEMPLE McPHERSON

_____

_____

_____

_____

_____

_____

_____

_____

_____

_____

_____

_____

_____

_____

_____

_____

_____

_____

_____

_____

_____

_____

_____

If ye abide in me, and my words abide in you, ye shall ask what ye will, ◄
and it shall be done unto you.

JOHN 15:7

▲ ▲ ▲

▼ ▼ ▼

► *"Faith never rises above its confession."*

— E. W. KENYON

_____

_____

_____

_____

_____

_____

_____

_____

_____

_____

_____

_____

_____

_____

_____

_____

_____

_____

_____

_____

► *Let us hold fast the confession of our hope without wavering, for He who promised is faithful.*

HEBREWS 10:23 *New American Standard*

▲ ▲ ▲

▼ ▼ ▼

"The God-kind of faith believes in the heart that what it says with the ◄
mouth will come to pass, and then dares to say it!"

— FREDERICK K.C. PRICE

_____

_____

_____

_____

_____

_____

_____

_____

_____

_____

_____

_____

_____

_____

_____

_____

_____

_____

_____

_____

_____

_____

Have faith that whatever you ask for in prayer is already granted you, ◄
and you will find it will be.

MARK 11:24 *Twentieth Century*

▲ ▲ ▲

▼ ▼ ▼

▶ *"Beloved, it is not our long prayers but our believing God that gets the answer."*

— JOHN G. LAKE

_____

_____

_____

_____

_____

_____

_____

_____

_____

_____

_____

_____

_____

_____

_____

_____

_____

_____

_____

_____

▶ *Because of this I say to you, all whatever — praying — ye do ask, believe that ye receive, and it shall be given to you.*

MARK 11:24 *Young*

▲ ▲ ▲

▼ ▼ ▼

"To be a good Christian, you must learn the secret of prayer." ◄
— BILLY GRAHAM

_____

_____

_____

_____

_____

_____

_____

_____

_____

_____

_____

_____

_____

_____

_____

_____

_____

_____

_____

_____

_____

Call to me, and I will answer you; I will tell you wonderful and ◄
marvelous things that you know nothing about.
JEREMIAH 33:3 *Good News*

▲ ▲ ▲

▼ ▼ ▼

► *"God wants us all to have an audacity of faith that dares to believe for all that is set forth in the Word."*

— SMITH WIGGLESWORTH

_____

_____

_____

_____

_____

_____

_____

_____

_____

_____

_____

_____

_____

_____

_____

_____

_____

_____

_____

_____

_____

► *For all the promises of God in him are yea, and in him Amen, unto the glory of God by us.*

2 CORINTHIANS 1:20

▲ ▲ ▲

▼ ▼ ▼

"The Lord longs to hear all of our concerns — any concern too small to ◀
be turned into a prayer is too small to be made into a burden."

— CORRIE TEN BOOM

_____

_____

_____

_____

_____

_____

_____

_____

_____

_____

_____

_____

_____

_____

_____

_____

_____

_____

_____

_____

_____

_____

_____

_____

But if there is anything you need, pray for it, asking God for it with ◀
prayer and thanksgiving.

PHILIPPIANS 4:6 *Jerusalem*

▲ ▲ ▲

▼ ▼ ▼

► *"The greatest power that God has given to any individual is the power of prayer."*

— KATHRYN KUHLMAN

_____

_____

_____

_____

_____

_____

_____

_____

_____

_____

_____

_____

_____

_____

_____

_____

_____

_____

_____

_____

► *For this reason I am telling you, whatever you ask for in prayer, believe (trust and be confident) that it is granted to you, and you will [get it].*
MARK 11:24 *Amplified*

▲ ▲ ▲

▼ ▼ ▼

"It is the knowledge of God's fatherliness revealed by the Holy Spirit ◄
that the power of prayer will take root and grow."

— ANDREW MURRAY

_____

_____

_____

_____

_____

_____

_____

_____

_____

_____

_____

_____

_____

_____

_____

_____

_____

_____

_____

_____

And I will pray the Father, and he shall give you another Comforter, ◄
that he may abide with you for ever; Even the Spirit of truth; whom
the world cannot receive, because it seeth him not, neither knoweth him:
but ye know him; for he dwelleth with you, and shall be in you.

JOHN 14:16, 17

▲ ▲ ▲

▼ ▼ ▼

► *"Praying in faith is merely having confidence in God's willingness to use His power to answer your prayer."*

— KENNETH COPELAND

_____

_____

_____

_____

_____

_____

_____

_____

_____

_____

_____

_____

_____

_____

_____

_____

_____

_____

_____

_____

_____

_____

► *And being fully persuaded that, what he had promised, he was able also to perform.*

ROMANS 4:21

▲ ▲ ▲

▼ ▼ ▼

"There are two kinds of Christians, those who pray their way through life, and those who butt their way through life."

— GORDON LINDSAY

In that day you will not ask me for anything. I tell you the truth, my Father will give you anything you ask for in my name.

JOHN 16:23 *New Century Version*

▲ ▲ ▲

▼ ▼ ▼

► *"By praying and standing in faith, the Christian builds a bridge for the weak person to come to God."*

— NORVEL HAYES

_____

_____

_____

_____

_____

_____

_____

_____

_____

_____

_____

_____

_____

_____

_____

_____

_____

_____

_____

► *But we will continue to devote ourselves steadfastly to prayer and the ministry of the Word.*

ACTS 6:4 *Amplified*

▲ ▲ ▲

▼ ▼ ▼

"Wishing will never be a substitute for prayer." ◄

— EDWIN LOUIS COLE

_____

_____

_____

_____

_____

_____

_____

_____

_____

_____

_____

_____

_____

_____

_____

_____

_____

_____

_____

_____

_____

_____

And whatever request you make in my name, that I will do, so that the ◄
Father may have glory in the Son.

JOHN 14:13 *Basic English*

▲ ▲ ▲

▼ ▼ ▼

► *"God has set a spiritual law before us. If we will learn to operate under the rules of His law, we will get our prayers answered."*

— CHARLES CAPPS

_____

_____

_____

_____

_____

_____

_____

_____

_____

_____

_____

_____

_____

_____

_____

_____

_____

_____

_____

_____

_____

► *Death and life are in the power of the tongue: and they that love it shall eat the fruit thereof.*

PROVERBS 18:21

▲ ▲ ▲

"A strange feature about this prayer life is that it reaches to the uttermost ◄
parts of the earth."

— E. W. KENYON

_____

_____

_____

_____

_____

_____

_____

_____

_____

_____

_____

_____

_____

_____

_____

_____

_____

_____

_____

_____

_____

_____

_____

_____

First of all, then, I urge that petitions, prayers, requests, and ◄
thanksgivings be offered to God for all people.

1 TIMOTHY 2:1 *Good News*

▼ ▼ ▼

► *"When I pray for a man in London or in Africa, my spirit can send to him through the Father, the blessing that he needs today."*

— E. W. KENYON

_____

_____

_____

_____

_____

_____

_____

_____

_____

_____

_____

_____

_____

_____

_____

_____

_____

_____

► *While he yet spake, there came from the ruler of the synagogue's house certain which said, Thy daughter is dead: why troublest thou the Master any further? As soon as Jesus heard the word that was spoken, he saith unto the ruler of the synagogue, Be not afraid, only believe.*

MARK 5:35, 36

▲ ▲ ▲

▼ ▼ ▼

"Whether we like it or not, asking is the rule of the kingdom."
— CHARLES H. SPURGEON ◄

_____

_____

_____

_____

_____

_____

_____

_____

_____

_____

_____

_____

_____

_____

_____

_____

_____

_____

_____

_____

_____

...ye have not, because ye ask not. ◄
JAMES 4:2

▲ ▲ ▲

▼ ▼ ▼

► *"It is impossible to measure up to God's purpose for our prayer life without being full of that Life that 'ever liveth to make intercession.'"*

— F. F. BOSWORTH

_____

_____

_____

_____

_____

_____

_____

_____

_____

_____

_____

_____

_____

_____

_____

_____

_____

_____

_____

_____

_____

_____

► *If you are in me at all times, and my words are in you, then anything for which you make a request will be done for you.*

JOHN 15:7 *Basic English*

▲ ▲ ▲

▼ ▼ ▼

"The failure of all Christian enterprise is a prayer failure." ◄

— E. W. KENYON

_____

_____

_____

_____

_____

_____

_____

_____

_____

_____

_____

_____

_____

_____

_____

_____

_____

_____

_____

_____

_____

_____

This book of the law shall not depart out of thy mouth; but thou shalt ◄
meditate therein day and night, that thou mayest observe to do
according to all that is written therein: for then thou shalt make thy
way prosperous, and then thou shalt have good success.

JOSHUA 1:8

▲ ▲ ▲

▼ ▼ ▼

► *"Unbelief demands material evidence rather than faith."*

— RAY MCCAULEY

_____

_____

_____

_____

_____

_____

_____

_____

_____

_____

_____

_____

_____

_____

_____

_____

_____

_____

_____

_____

_____

_____

_____

► *Now faith is an assurance of things hoped for, a sure persuasion of things not seen.*

HEBREWS 11:1 *Worrell*

▲ ▲ ▲

▼ ▼ ▼

"A doubter often prays for things he already possesses." ◄

— T. L. OSBORN

_____

_____

_____

_____

_____

_____

_____

_____

_____

_____

_____

_____

_____

_____

_____

_____

_____

_____

For verily I say unto you, That whosoever shall say unto this ◄
mountain, Be thou removed, and be thou cast into the sea; and shall not
doubt in his heart, but shall believe that those things which he saith
shall come to pass; he shall have whatsoever he saith.

MARK 11:23

▲ ▲ ▲

▼ ▼ ▼

► *"What is the secret of prayer? What is the secret of moving mountains by the prayer of faith? The first thing is to recognize the presence of Him Who created mountains."*

— GORDON LINDSAY

_____

_____

_____

_____

_____

_____

_____

_____

_____

_____

_____

_____

_____

_____

_____

_____

_____

_____

► *Come now! Do you not understand, have you not heard, that the Eternal is an everlasting God, the maker of the world from end to end? He never faints, never is weary, his insight is unsearchable.*

ISAIAH 40:28 *Moffatt*

▲ ▲ ▲

▼ ▼ ▼

"If I fail to spend two hours in prayer each morning, the devil gets the ◄
victory through the day."

— MARTIN LUTHER

_____

_____

_____

_____

_____

_____

_____

_____

_____

_____

_____

_____

_____

_____

_____

_____

_____

_____

_____

_____

_____

And in the morning, rising up a great while before day, he went out, ◄
and departed into a solitary place, and there prayed.

MARK 1:35

▲ ▲ ▲

▼ ▼ ▼

► *"I never saw a man get anything from God who prayed on earth. If you get anything from God, you will have to pray into heaven for it is all there."*

— SMITH WIGGLESWORTH

_____

_____

_____

_____

_____

_____

_____

_____

_____

_____

_____

_____

_____

_____

_____

_____

_____

_____

_____

► *Then you will call my name. You will come to me and pray to me, and I will listen to you.*

JEREMIAH 29:12 *New Century Version*

▲ ▲ ▲

▼ ▼ ▼

"When you pray for others, it is as if you went and stood beside the Lord ◄
and together you talked about their needs."

— CORRIE TEN BOOM

_____

_____

_____

_____

_____

_____

_____

_____

_____

_____

_____

_____

_____

_____

_____

_____

_____

_____

_____

_____

_____

Have faith that whatever you ask for in prayer is already granted you, ◄
and you will find that it will be.

MARK 11:24 *Twentieth Century*

▲ ▲ ▲

▼ ▼ ▼

► *"When it comes to making major changes it's better to be too slow than too fast because it's easier to play catch up than clean up."*

— BUDDY HARRISON

_____

_____

_____

_____

_____

_____

_____

_____

_____

_____

_____

_____

_____

_____

_____

_____

_____

_____

_____

_____

► *But they that wait upon the Lord shall renew their strength; they shall mount up with wings as eagles; they shall run, and not be weary; and they shall walk, and not faint.*

ISAIAH 40:31

▲ ▲ ▲

▼ ▼ ▼

"Your children learn more of your faith during the bad times than they ◄
do during the good times."

— BEVERLY LaHAYE

_____

_____

_____

_____

_____

_____

_____

_____

_____

_____

_____

_____

_____

_____

_____

_____

_____

_____

_____

Reckon it nothing but joy, my brethren, whenever you find yourselves ◄
hedged in by various trials. Be assured that the testing of your faith
leads to power of endurance. Only let endurance have perfect results so
that you may become perfect and complete, deficient in nothing.

JAMES 1:2-4 *Weymouth*

▲ ▲ ▲

▼ ▼ ▼

► *"To spend little time with Jesus is to accomplish little in Jesus."*

— CAROLYN SAVELLE

_____

_____

_____

_____

_____

_____

_____

_____

_____

_____

_____

_____

_____

_____

_____

_____

_____

_____

_____

_____

► *If you remain in me and my words remain in you, ask whatever you wish, and it will be given you.*

JOHN 15:7 *New International Version*

▲ ▲ ▲

▼ ▼ ▼

"Take a stand of faith and say, 'Devil, you are a liar. I am going to ◄
believe God for a miracle because He is going to turn this situation
around.'"

— R. W. SCHAMBACH

_____

_____

_____

_____

_____

_____

_____

_____

_____

_____

_____

_____

_____

_____

_____

_____

_____

_____

_____

_____

Finally, be strong in the Lord, and in the strength of His might. Put on ◄
the whole armor of God, that ye may be able to stand against the wiles
of the Devil.

EPHESIANS 6:10,11 *Worrell*

...he [the devil] is a liar.

JOHN 8:44

▲ ▲ ▲

▼ ▼ ▼

▶ *"The simplest soul can touch God and live in the very presence of the Almighty."*

—JOHN G. LAKE

_____

_____

_____

_____

_____

_____

_____

_____

_____

_____

_____

_____

_____

_____

_____

_____

_____

_____

_____

_____

▶ *The Lord is not slack concerning his promise, as some men count slackness; but is longsuffering to us-ward, not willing that any should perish, but that all should come to repentance.*

2 PETER 3:9

...lo, I am with you alway, even unto the end of the world. Amen.

MATTHEW 28:20

▲ ▲ ▲

▼ ▼ ▼

"God puts no restriction on faith; faith puts no restriction on God." ◀

— JOHN L. MASON

_____

_____

_____

_____

_____

_____

_____

_____

_____

_____

_____

_____

_____

_____

_____

_____

_____

_____

_____

_____

_____

_____

But to the Power able to do all, far beyond what we can ask or think, ◀
by means of His power energizing in us.

EPHESIANS 3:20 *Fenton*

▲ ▲ ▲

▼ ▼ ▼

► *"You can't build a prayer life just praying alone. It has to be built upon God's Word."*

— KENNETH E. HAGIN

_____

_____

_____

_____

_____

_____

_____

_____

_____

_____

_____

_____

_____

_____

_____

_____

_____

_____

_____

_____

_____

► *My son, attend to what I say, bend your ear to my words; never lose sight of them, but fix them in your mind.*

PROVERBS 4:20,21 *Moffatt*

▲ ▲ ▲

▼ ▼ ▼

"Persevere, let the Word and the Spirit teach you to pray."   ◄

— ANDREW MURRAY

_____

_____

_____

_____

_____

_____

_____

_____

_____

_____

_____

_____

_____

_____

_____

_____

_____

_____

_____

_____

_____

We don't know how we should pray, but the Spirit helps our weakness. ◄
He personally talks to God for us with feelings which our language
cannot express.

ROMANS 8:26 *Simple English Bible*

▲ ▲ ▲

▼ ▼ ▼

► *"The key to success in prayer is expecting results."*

— KENNETH COPELAND

_____

_____

_____

_____

_____

_____

_____

_____

_____

_____

_____

_____

_____

_____

_____

_____

_____

_____

_____

_____

_____

_____

► *That is why I tell you, as to whatever you pray and make request for, if you believe that you have received it it shall be yours.*

MARK 11:24 *Weymouth*

▲ ▲ ▲

▼ ▼ ▼

"Everything we do or say apart from love is a step in darkness." ◀

— PAT HARRISON

_____

_____

_____

_____

_____

_____

_____

_____

_____

_____

_____

_____

_____

_____

_____

_____

_____

_____

_____

_____

He that loveth his brother abideth in the light, and there is none ◀
occasion of stumbling in him. But he that hateth his brother is in
darkness, and walketh in darkness, and knoweth not whither he goeth,
because that darkness hath blinded his eyes.

1 JOHN 2:10,11

▲ ▲ ▲

▼ ▼ ▼

► *"That natural and the supernatural coming together make an explosive force for God."*

— KENNETH HAGIN JR.

_____

_____

_____

_____

_____

_____

_____

_____

_____

_____

_____

_____

_____

_____

_____

_____

_____

_____

_____

_____

_____

_____

_____

_____

► *Behold, I have given you the authority to tread upon serpents and scorpions, and over all the power of the enemy; and nothing shall in any wise harm you.*

LUKE 10:19 *Worrell*

▲ ▲ ▲

▼ ▼ ▼

"You'll never win a battle on the shells you fired in the last war. When ◀
a new enemy comes, it's time to reload."

— CREFLO A. DOLLAR, JR.

_____

_____

_____

_____

_____

_____

_____

_____

_____

_____

_____

_____

_____

_____

_____

_____

_____

_____

_____

_____

_____

◀

...we are not ignorant of his [Satan's] schemes.
2 CORINTHIANS 2:11 *New American Standard*

▲ ▲ ▲

▼ ▼ ▼

► *"God does not give victory over the world just to a select few. He has given overcoming victory to every person that is born again."*

— BILLY JOE DAUGHERTY

_____

_____

_____

_____

_____

_____

_____

_____

_____

_____

_____

_____

_____

_____

_____

_____

_____

_____

_____

_____

_____

► *For whatever is born of God overcomes the world. And this is the victory that has overcome the world — our faith.*

1 JOHN 5:4 *New King James Version*

▲ ▲ ▲

▼ ▼ ▼

"When the storms of life strike, it's what happens 'in' you that will ◄
determine what happens 'to' you."

— JERRY SAVELLE

_____

_____

_____

_____

_____

_____

_____

_____

_____

_____

_____

_____

_____

_____

_____

_____

_____

_____

_____

_____

_____

While our minds are not on the things which are seen, but on the things ◄
which are not seen: for the things which are seen are for a time; but the
things which are not seen are eternal.

2 CORINTHIANS 4:18 *Basic English*

▲ ▲ ▲

▼ ▼ ▼

► *"The Word of God becomes the thing men live by, the thing men will die for, when the Word of God becomes a present, living reality."*
— JOHN G. LAKE

_____

_____

_____

_____

_____

_____

_____

_____

_____

_____

_____

_____

_____

_____

_____

_____

_____

_____

_____

_____

_____

_____

► *It is the spirit that quickeneth; the flesh profiteth nothing: the words that I speak unto you, they are spirit, and they are life.*
JOHN 6:63

▲ ▲ ▲

"I am not moved by what I see or hear; I am moved by what I believe." ◄
— SMITH WIGGLESWORTH

_____

_____

_____

_____

_____

_____

_____

_____

_____

_____

_____

_____

_____

_____

_____

_____

_____

_____

_____

_____

For we walk by faith [we regulate our lives and conduct ourselves by ◄
our conviction or belief respecting man's relationship to God and divine
things, with trust and holy fervor; thus we walk] not by sight or
appearance.

2 CORINTHIANS 5:7 *Amplified*

▼ ▼ ▼

▶ *"Prayer has two pillars, Trust and Faith."*

— CHARLES NEIMAN

_____

_____

_____

_____

_____

_____

_____

_____

_____

_____

_____

_____

_____

_____

_____

_____

_____

_____

_____

_____

_____

▶ *For this reason I say to you, Whatever you make a request for in prayer,*
have faith that it has been given to you, and you will have it.
MARK 11:24 *Basic English*

▲ ▲ ▲

▼ ▼ ▼

"Prayer is both asking and receiving, speaking and listening. You can ◄
learn how to converse with God."

— CORRIE TEN BOOM

_____

_____

_____

_____

_____

_____

_____

_____

_____

_____

_____

_____

_____

_____

_____

_____

_____

_____

_____

_____

_____

_____

Ask, and it will be given to you; seek, and you will find; knock, and it ◄
will be opened to you. For everyone who asks receives, and he who seeks
finds, and to him who knocks it will be opened.

MATTHEW 7:7 *New King James Version*

Be still, and know that I am God: I will be exalted among the heathen,
I will be exalted in the earth.

PSALM 46:10

▲ ▲ ▲

▼ ▼ ▼

► *"One with God is a majority."*

— BILLY GRAHAM

_____

_____

_____

_____

_____

_____

_____

_____

_____

_____

_____

_____

_____

_____

_____

_____

_____

_____

_____

_____

_____

► *What, then, shall we say in response to this? If God is for us, who can be against us?*

ROMANS 8:31 *New International Version*

▲ ▲ ▲

▼ ▼ ▼

"This power does not work just as dynamite to bring one explosive ◄
experience in your life. It is continual power."

— JOHN OSTEEN

_____

_____

_____

_____

_____

_____

_____

_____

_____

_____

_____

_____

_____

_____

_____

_____

_____

_____

_____

_____

_____

_____

...The earnest (heartfelt, continued) prayer of a righteous man makes ◄
tremendous power available [dynamic in its working].

JAMES 5:16 *Amplified*

▲ ▲ ▲

▼ ▼ ▼

► *"A consistent prayer life is absolutely indispensable, if we wish to surmount serious troubles and perhaps tragedies, building up against us in the future."*

— GORDON LINDSAY

_____

_____

_____

_____

_____

_____

_____

_____

_____

_____

_____

_____

_____

_____

_____

_____

_____

_____

_____

_____

_____

► *Pray continually.*

1 THESSALONIANS 5:17 *New Century Version*

▲ ▲ ▲

▼ ▼ ▼

"The greatest thing you will ever learn about intercessory prayer, the ◄
greatest help, is to depend on the Holy Spirit."

— ED DUFRESNE

Pray with unceasing prayer and entreaty on every fitting occasion in ◄
the Spirit, and be always on the alert to seize opportunities for doing so,
with unwearied persistence and entreaty on behalf of all God's people.
EPHESIANS 6:18 *Weymouth*

▲ ▲ ▲

▼ ▼ ▼

► *"Thinking faith thoughts and speaking faith words will lead your heart out of defeat and into victory."*

— KENNETH E. HAGIN

_____

_____

_____

_____

_____

_____

_____

_____

_____

_____

_____

_____

_____

_____

_____

_____

_____

_____

_____

_____

_____

_____

► *Whoso keepeth his mouth and his tongue keepeth his soul from troubles.*
PROVERBS 21:23

▲ ▲ ▲

▼ ▼ ▼

"Real prayer is head and heart conversation with God."

— ROY HICKS ◄

_____

_____

_____

_____

_____

_____

_____

_____

_____

_____

_____

_____

_____

_____

_____

_____

_____

_____

_____

_____

_____

_____

_____

Let the words of my mouth, and the meditation of my heart, be ◄
acceptable in thy sight, O Lord, my strength, and my redeemer.

PSALM 19:14

▲ ▲ ▲

▼ ▼ ▼

► *"Prayer is the 'living' Word in our mouth. Our mouth must speak faith, for faith is what pleases God."*

— CAROLYN EAST, WORD MINISTRIES

_____

_____

_____

_____

_____

_____

_____

_____

_____

_____

_____

_____

_____

_____

_____

_____

_____

_____

_____

► *But without faith it is impossible to please and be satisfactory to Him. For whoever would come near to God must [necessarily] believe that God exists and that He is the rewarder of those who earnestly and diligently seek Him [out].*

HEBREWS 11:6 *Amplified*

▲ ▲ ▲

▼ ▼ ▼

"Prayer flows out of a renewed relationship with Christ, a communion ◄
with God based upon love and trust in Him to be our all-sufficiency."

— ANDREW MURRAY

_____

_____

_____

_____

_____

_____

_____

_____

_____

_____

_____

_____

_____

_____

_____

_____

_____

_____

_____

_____

_____

_____

_____

_____

_____

May the words of my mouth always find favour, and the whispering of ◄
my heart, in your presence, Yahweh, my Rock, my Redeemer!

PSALM 19:14 *Jerusalem*

▲ ▲ ▲

▼ ▼ ▼

► *"Now you have returned God's Word to Him and He said that it will not return to Him void. He will perform it."*

— CHARLES CAPPS

_____

_____

_____

_____

_____

_____

_____

_____

_____

_____

_____

_____

_____

_____

_____

_____

_____

_____

_____

_____

► *So shall my word be that goeth forth out of my mouth: it shall not return unto me void, but it shall accomplish that which I please, and it shall prosper in the thing whereto I sent it.*

ISAIAH 55:11

▲ ▲ ▲

▼ ▼ ▼

"The prayer habit will be born of your own will." ◄

— E. W. KENYON

_____

_____

_____

_____

_____

_____

_____

_____

_____

_____

_____

_____

_____

_____

_____

_____

_____

_____

_____

_____

_____

_____

Pray with unceasing prayer and entreaty on every fitting occasion in the Spirit, and be always on the alert to seize opportunities for doing so, ◄ *with unwearied persistence and entreaty on behalf of all God's people.*
EPHESIANS 6:18 *Weymouth*

▲ ▲ ▲

▼ ▼ ▼

► *"We will go only as far with God as we're willing to go in prayer."*

— LARRY LEA

_____

_____

_____

_____

_____

_____

_____

_____

_____

_____

_____

_____

_____

_____

_____

_____

_____

_____

_____

_____

_____

► *Be persistent in prayer, and keep alert as you pray, giving thanks to God.*

COLOSSIANS 4:2 *Good News*

▲ ▲ ▲

▼ ▼ ▼

"Fear is the reverse gear of faith. Fear releases the ability of Satan ◄
against you. Faith releases the ability of God on your behalf."

— CHARLES CAPPS

_____

_____

_____

_____

_____

_____

_____

_____

_____

_____

_____

_____

_____

_____

_____

_____

_____

_____

_____

_____

_____

_____

And he saith unto them, Why are ye fearful, O ye of little faith? Then ◄
he arose, and rebuked the winds and the sea; and there was a great calm.

MATTHEW 8:26

▲ ▲ ▲

▼ ▼ ▼

► *"Jesus really gives us the power of attorney. That means that what Jesus can do, we can do."*

— KENNETH E. HAGIN

_____

_____

_____

_____

_____

_____

_____

_____

_____

_____

_____

_____

_____

_____

_____

_____

_____

_____

_____

_____

► *And Jesus came and spake unto them, saying, All power is given unto me in heaven and in earth.*

MATTHEW 28:18

Behold, I give unto you power to tread on serpents and scorpions, and over all the power of the enemy: and nothing shall by any means hurt you.

LUKE 10:19

▲ ▲ ▲

▼ ▼ ▼

"When we pray to be quickened 'according to the Word' we know that ◄
we are praying according to His will and can therefore obtain the
answer."

— F. F. BOSWORTH

_____

_____

_____

_____

_____

_____

_____

_____

_____

_____

_____

_____

_____

_____

_____

_____

_____

_____

_____

_____

_____

_____

_____

I am afflicted very much: quicken me, O Lord, according unto thy word. ◄
PSALM 119:107

▲ ▲ ▲

▼ ▼ ▼

► *"If we seek to feed the fire of our prayers with the fuel of God's Word, all our difficulties in prayer will disappear."*

— R. A. TORREY

_____

_____

_____

_____

_____

_____

_____

_____

_____

_____

_____

_____

_____

_____

_____

_____

_____

_____

_____

_____

_____

► *If you live in Me [abide vitally united to Me] and My words remain in you and continue to live in your hearts, ask whatever you will, and it shall be done for you.*

JOHN 15:7 *Amplified*

▲ ▲ ▲

▼ ▼ ▼

"Don't hesitate to pray for someone on the street or in a restaurant. The ◄
whole world is your turf. Dominate it!"

— MIKE MURDOCK

_____

_____

_____

_____

_____

_____

_____

_____

_____

_____

_____

_____

_____

_____

_____

_____

_____

_____

_____

_____

_____

_____

Then Jesus came forward to them and said, "Full authority has been ◄
given to me in heaven and on earth; go and make disciples of all
nations, baptize them in the name of the Father and the Son and the
holy Spirit.

MATTHEW 28:18, 19 *Moffatt*

▲ ▲ ▲

▼ ▼ ▼

► *"If we expect to accomplish great things, then we must maintain constant communication and fellowship with God."*

— JERRY SAVELLE

_____

_____

_____

_____

_____

_____

_____

_____

_____

_____

_____

_____

_____

_____

_____

_____

_____

_____

_____

_____

► *You must pray at all times as the Holy Spirit leads you to pray. Pray for the things that are needed. You must watch and keep on praying. Remember to pray for all Christians.*

EPHESIANS 6:18 *New Life Version*

▲ ▲ ▲

▼ ▼ ▼

"Start today recognizing and practicing the presence of Christ in your ◄
life."

— GORDON LINDSAY

_____

_____

_____

_____

_____

_____

_____

_____

_____

_____

_____

_____

_____

_____

_____

_____

_____

_____

That he would grant you, according to the riches of his glory, to be
strengthened with might by his Spirit in the inner man; that Christ
may dwell in your hearts by faith; that ye, being rooted and grounded
in love, may be able to comprehend with all saints what is the breadth,
and length, and depth, and height; and to know the love of Christ,
which passeth knowledge, that ye might be filled with all the fulness of ◄
God.

EPHESIANS 3:16-19

▲ ▲ ▲

▼ ▼ ▼

► *"He that has prayed well has studied well."*

— MARTIN LUTHER

_____

_____

_____

_____

_____

_____

_____

_____

_____

_____

_____

_____

_____

_____

_____

_____

_____

_____

_____

_____

_____

► *Study to shew thyself approved unto God, a workman that needeth not to be ashamed, rightly dividing the word of truth.*
2 TIMOTHY 2:15

▲ ▲ ▲

▼ ▼ ▼

"God channels all the power of heaven through the authority of the ◄
believer who knows the rights and privileges that belong to him and are
found in the name of Jesus."

— BOB YANDIAN

_____

_____

_____

_____

_____

_____

_____

_____

_____

_____

_____

_____

_____

_____

_____

_____

_____

_____

_____

I assure you, most solemnly I tell you, if anyone steadfastly believes in Me, ◄
he will himself be able to do the things that I do; and he will do even
greater things than these, because I go to the Father. And I will do [I Myself
will grant] whatever you ask in My Name [as presenting all that I AM],
so that the Father may be glorified and extolled in (through) the Son.

JOHN 14:12, 13 *Amplified*

▲ ▲ ▲

▼ ▼ ▼

► *"It's hard for God to walk with a man who gets his mind made up to do things his own way."*

— NORVEL HAYES

_____

_____

_____

_____

_____

_____

_____

_____

_____

_____

_____

_____

_____

_____

_____

_____

_____

_____

_____

_____

_____

► *Trust in the Lord with all thine heart; and lean not unto thine own understanding. In all thy ways acknowledge him, and he shall direct thy paths.*

PROVERBS 3:5, 6

▲ ▲ ▲

▼ ▼ ▼

"God has made you and me that our inner man should stand up tall and ◄
not faint in the midst of the problems of life."

— ORAL ROBERTS

_____

_____

_____

_____

_____

_____

_____

_____

_____

_____

_____

_____

_____

_____

_____

_____

_____

_____

_____

_____

_____

_____

_____

_____

And he spake a parable unto them to this end, that men ought always ◄
to pray, and not to faint.

LUKE 18:1

▲ ▲ ▲

▼ ▼ ▼

► *"The greatest thing one person can do for another is to pray for him."*
— CORRIE TEN BOOM

_____

_____

_____

_____

_____

_____

_____

_____

_____

_____

_____

_____

_____

_____

_____

_____

_____

_____

_____

_____

► *My desire is, first of all, that you will make requests and prayers and give praise for all men.*

1 TIMOTHY 2:1 *Basic English*

▲ ▲ ▲

▼ ▼ ▼

"Sometimes God doesn't tell us His plan because we wouldn't believe it anyway."

— CARLTON PEARSON

_____

_____

_____

_____

_____

_____

_____

_____

_____

_____

_____

_____

_____

_____

_____

_____

_____

_____

_____

_____

_____

Now to him who is able to do immeasurably more than all we ask or imagine, according to his power that is at work within us.

EPHESIANS 3:20 *New International Version*

▲ ▲ ▲

▼ ▼ ▼

► *"Let us unite...in imploring the Supreme Ruler of nations to spread His holy protection over these United States."*

— GEORGE WASHINGTON

_____

_____

_____

_____

_____

_____

_____

_____

_____

_____

_____

_____

_____

_____

_____

_____

_____

_____

_____

_____

_____

_____

► *When my People; upon whom My Name is invoked, kneel and pray, and seek My Presence, and turn from their wicked courses, then I will listen, and forgive their sins, and will restore health to their land.*

2 CHRONICLES 7:14 *Fenton*

▲ ▲ ▲

▼ ▼ ▼

"Prayer is facing God with man's needs, with His promise to meet those needs." ◄

— E. W. KENYON

_____

_____

_____

_____

_____

_____

_____

_____

_____

_____

_____

_____

_____

_____

_____

_____

_____

_____

_____

_____

_____

_____

_____

_____

_____

_____

_____

And I will do whatever you ask for in my name, so that the Father's glory will be shown through the Son. ◄

JOHN 14:13 *Good News*

▲ ▲ ▲

▼ ▼ ▼

► *"Think what it would mean in your prayer life if you were strengthened with all might to call upon God each day!"*

— ANDREW MURRAY

_____

_____

_____

_____

_____

_____

_____

_____

_____

_____

_____

_____

_____

_____

_____

_____

_____

_____

_____

_____

_____

_____

► *Strengthened with all power, according to His glorious might, for the attaining of all steadfastness and patience.*

COLOSSIANS 1:11 *New American Standard*

▲ ▲ ▲

"God has only prepared one kind of life for us, and that is the abundant life." ◄

— NORVEL HAYES

Now unto him that is able to do exceeding abundantly above all that ◄
we ask or think, according to the power that worketh in us.
EPHESIANS 3:20

▼ ▼ ▼

► *"Faith is believing that what you cannot see will come to pass."*
— EDWIN LOUIS COLE

_____

_____

_____

_____

_____

_____

_____

_____

_____

_____

_____

_____

_____

_____

_____

_____

_____

_____

_____

_____

_____

_____

► *So we fix our eyes not on what is seen, but on what is unseen. For what is seen is temporary, but what is unseen is eternal.*
2 CORINTHIANS 4:18 *New International Version*

▲ ▲ ▲

"Worship is man's total being aglow in the life the Holy Spirit imparts, offering spiritual sacrifices."

— JACK HAYFORD

_____

_____

_____

_____

_____

_____

_____

_____

_____

_____

_____

_____

_____

_____

_____

_____

_____

_____

_____

_____

_____

_____

Let my prayer be set forth before thee as incense; and the lifting up of my hands as the evening sacrifice.

PSALM 141:2·

▼ ▼ ▼

► *"Waiting is where the battle is won in the spiritual realm. Waiting and keeping our eyes on God."*

—JOYCE MEYER

_____

_____

_____

_____

_____

_____

_____

_____

_____

_____

_____

_____

_____

_____

_____

_____

_____

_____

_____

_____

► *But let patience have its perfect work, that you may be perfect and complete, lacking nothing.*

JAMES 1:4 *New King James Version*

▲ ▲ ▲

▼ ▼ ▼

"I seek the will of the Spirit of God through the Word of God. The Spirit ◄
and the Word must be combined."

— GEORGE MUELLER

_____

_____

_____

_____

_____

_____

_____

_____

_____

_____

_____

_____

_____

_____

_____

_____

_____

_____

_____

_____

_____

_____

And this is the boldness that we have toward Him, that if anything we ◄
may ask according to his will, He doth hear us.

1 JOHN 5:14 *Young*

▲ ▲ ▲

▼ ▼ ▼

► *"Faith opens the door to God's promise for you; and patience keeps it open until that promise is fulfilled."*

— KENNETH COPELAND

► *That ye be not slothful, but followers of them who through faith and patience inherit the promises.*

HEBREWS 6:12

▲ ▲ ▲

▼ ▼ ▼

"Jesus called people by their first names. He recognized them as individuals and answered their prayers."

— ORAL ROBERTS

_____

_____

_____

_____

_____

_____

_____

_____

_____

_____

_____

_____

_____

_____

_____

_____

_____

_____

_____

_____

_____

_____

And whatsoever ye shall ask in my name, that will I do, that the Father may be glorified in the Son.

JOHN 14:13

▲ ▲ ▲

▼ ▼ ▼

► *"Do not assume that your faith is always in top-notch shape! Rather, plan it safe and assume that your faith always needs a fresh anointing."*

— RICK RENNER

_____

_____

_____

_____

_____

_____

_____

_____

_____

_____

_____

_____

_____

_____

_____

_____

_____

_____

_____

_____

_____

► *So then faith cometh by hearing, and hearing by the word of God.*

ROMANS 10:17

▲ ▲ ▲

▼ ▼ ▼

"Need is not what moves God; faith does. Vain repetitions do not move ◄
God; faith does. Much speaking does not move God; faith does."

— CHARLES CAPPS

_____

_____

_____

_____

_____

_____

_____

_____

_____

_____

_____

_____

_____

_____

_____

_____

_____

_____

_____

_____

_____

_____

_____

Therefore I am saying to you, All, whatever you are praying and ◄
requesting, be believing that you obtained, and it will be yours.

MARK 11:24 *Concordant Literal*

▲ ▲ ▲

▼ ▼ ▼

► *"Pray to the place where peace rules in your soul."*

— GORDON LINDSAY

_____

_____

_____

_____

_____

_____

_____

_____

_____

_____

_____

_____

_____

_____

_____

_____

_____

_____

_____

_____

► *Have no cares; but in everything with prayer and praise put your requests before God. And the peace of God, which is deeper than all knowledge, will keep your hearts and minds in Christ Jesus.*

PHILIPPIANS 4:6, 7 *Basic English*

▲ ▲ ▲

"God can and will give us victory if we only trust Him." ◄
— MARIA WOODWORTH-ETTER

I will say of the Lord, "He is my refuge and my fortress, my God, in ◄
whom I trust." A thousand my fall at your side, ten thousand at your
right hand, but it will not come near you.

PSALM 91:2, 7 *New International Version*

▲ ▲ ▲

▼ ▼ ▼

► *"The reason God is unable to bless His people with abundance is because most have their hands gripped on their own meager substances."*

— JESSE DUPLANTIS

_____

_____

_____

_____

_____

_____

_____

_____

_____

_____

_____

_____

_____

_____

_____

_____

_____

_____

_____

► *Give, and [gifts] will be given to you; good measure, pressed down, shaken together, and running over, will they pour into [the pouch formed by] the bosom [of your robe and used as a bag]. For with the measure you deal out [with the measure you use when you confer benefits on others], it will be measured back to you.*

LUKE 6:38 *Amplified*

▲ ▲ ▲

▼ ▼ ▼

"A prayer accurately formed and stated from the Word of God will ◄
absolutely move heaven, earth, and the things under the earth in your
behalf."

— CHARLES CAPPS

_____

_____

_____

_____

_____

_____

_____

_____

_____

_____

_____

_____

_____

_____

_____

_____

_____

_____

_____

_____

So shall my word be that goeth forth out of my mouth: it shall not return ◄
unto me void, but it shall accomplish that which I please, and it shall
prosper in the thing whereto I sent it.

ISAIAH 55:11

▲ ▲ ▲

▼ ▼ ▼

► *"As a camel kneels before his master to have him remove his burden at the end of the day, so kneel each night and let the Master take your burden."*

— CORRIE TEN BOOM

_____

_____

_____

_____

_____

_____

_____

_____

_____

_____

_____

_____

_____

_____

_____

_____

_____

_____

_____

_____

► *Putting all your troubles on him, for he takes care of you.*
1 PETER 5:7 *Basic English*

▲ ▲ ▲

▼ ▼ ▼

"When you enter into prayer, search your heart. God may have ◄ something He wants you to do."

— ORAL ROBERTS

_____

_____

_____

_____

_____

_____

_____

_____

_____

_____

_____

_____

_____

_____

_____

_____

_____

_____

_____

_____

_____

_____

_____

_____

_____

After the earthquake a fire, but the Eternal was not in the fire; after the ◄ fire the breath of a light whisper.

1 KINGS 19:12 *Moffatt*

▲ ▲ ▲

▼ ▼ ▼

► *"He can give only according to His might; therefore He always gives more than we ask for."*

— MARTIN LUTHER

_____

_____

_____

_____

_____

_____

_____

_____

_____

_____

_____

_____

_____

_____

_____

_____

_____

_____

_____

_____

_____

_____

► *Now to Him who, in exercise of His power that is at work within us, is able to do infinitely beyond all our highest prayers or thoughts.*

EPHESIANS 3:20 *Weymouth*

▲ ▲ ▲

▼ ▼ ▼

"Agreement makes prayer work." ◄

— KENNETH COPELAND

_____

_____

_____

_____

_____

_____

_____

_____

_____

_____

_____

_____

_____

_____

_____

_____

_____

_____

_____

_____

_____

_____

Again I say unto you, That if two of you shall agree on earth as touching ◄
any thing that they shall ask, it shall be done for them of my Father
which is in heaven.

MATTHEW 18:19

▲ ▲ ▲

▼ ▼ ▼

► *"When I use the faith I have, God not only answers that but goes an extra step and gives things I could only imagine."*

— BOB YANDIAN

_____

_____

_____

_____

_____

_____

_____

_____

_____

_____

_____

_____

_____

_____

_____

_____

_____

_____

_____

_____

► *Now to Him Who is able to do superexcessively above all that we are requesting or apprehending, according to the power that is operating in us.*
EPHESIANS 3:20 *Concordant Literal*

▲ ▲ ▲

▼ ▼ ▼

"To be possessed with an ever increasing faith one must make constant ◄
use of the faith that they have."

— CHARLES S. PRICE

_____

_____

_____

_____

_____

_____

_____

_____

_____

_____

_____

_____

_____

_____

_____

_____

_____

_____

_____

_____

_____

_____

But wilt thou know, O vain man, that faith without works is dead? ◄
JAMES 2:20

▲ ▲ ▲

▼ ▼ ▼

► *"Real faith in God — heart faith — believes the Word of God regardless of what the physical evidence may be."*

— KENNETH E. HAGIN

_____

_____

_____

_____

_____

_____

_____

_____

_____

_____

_____

_____

_____

_____

_____

_____

_____

_____

_____

► *While we look not at the things that are seen, but at the things that are not seen; for the things that are seen are temporal, but the things that are unseen are eternal.*

2 CORINTHIANS 4:18 *Worrell*

▲ ▲ ▲

▼ ▼ ▼

"You are a child of destiny. God is orchestrating and ordaining your ◄
steps and your life — if you are yielded to Him."

— CARLTON PEARSON

_____

_____

_____

_____

_____

_____

_____

_____

_____

_____

_____

_____

_____

_____

_____

_____

_____

_____

_____

_____

_____

_____

_____

The steps of a [good] man are directed and established by the Lord when ◄
He delights in his way [and He busies Himself with his every step].

PSALM 37:23 *Amplified*

▲ ▲ ▲

▼ ▼ ▼

► *"Payday doesn't come every Saturday night, but if you are faithful to God and His Word, payday always comes."*

— ORETHA HAGIN

_____

_____

_____

_____

_____

_____

_____

_____

_____

_____

_____

_____

_____

_____

_____

_____

_____

_____

_____

_____

_____

_____

► *A faithful man shall abound with blessings: but he that maketh haste to be rich shall not be innocent.*

PROVERBS 28:20

▲ ▲ ▲

▼ ▼ ▼

"Absorb the principle that failure is never final, so if you do not succeed ◄
the first time, keep on trying."

— DAISY OSBORN

_____

_____

_____

_____

_____

_____

_____

_____

_____

_____

_____

_____

_____

_____

_____

_____

_____

_____

_____

_____

_____

And let us not be weary in well doing: for in due season we shall reap, ◄
if we faint not.

GALATIANS 6:9

▲ ▲ ▲

▼ ▼ ▼

► *"The successful prayer life is one of self-denial. It is a recognition of His Lordship, a giving up of much that is not wrong in itself, but that hinders and takes our time."*

— E. W. KENYON

_____

_____

_____

_____

_____

_____

_____

_____

_____

_____

_____

_____

_____

_____

_____

_____

_____

_____

_____

► *Wherefore seeing we also are compassed about with so great a cloud of witnesses, let us lay aside every weight, and the sin which doth so easily beset us, and let us run with patience the race that is set before us.*

HEBREWS 12:1

▲ ▲ ▲

▼ ▼ ▼

"He that waits to pray, or who loses heart in prayer because he does not ◄
yet feel the faith needed to get the answer, will never learn to believe."
— ANDREW MURRAY

_____

_____

_____

_____

_____

_____

_____

_____

_____

_____

_____

_____

_____

_____

_____

_____

_____

_____

_____

_____

_____

_____

For we walk by faith, not by sight. ◄

2 CORINTHIANS 5:7

▲ ▲ ▲

▼ ▼ ▼

► *"The result of prayer in private will be a life of boldness and courage in public."*

— EDWIN LOUIS COLE

_____

_____

_____

_____

_____

_____

_____

_____

_____

_____

_____

_____

_____

_____

_____

_____

_____

_____

_____

_____

_____

_____

► *And he withdrew into solitary places, and prayed.*
LUKE 5:16 *Living Oracles*

▲ ▲ ▲

▼ ▼ ▼

"God wants His people hot. He wants them growing and moving. He ◄ wants them striving for the best and pressing on."

— CASEY TREAT

_____

_____

_____

_____

_____

_____

_____

_____

_____

_____

_____

_____

_____

_____

_____

_____

_____

_____

_____

_____

_____

_____

Therefore, having so great a cloud of witnesses surrounding us — ◄ having thrown off every encumbrance and the easily besetting sin — let us run with patience the race lying before us.

HEBREWS 12:1 *Worrell*

▲ ▲ ▲

▼ ▼ ▼

► *"God answers prayer because He is your Father; you are His son and you have a covenant with Him."*

— CHARLES CAPPS

_____

_____

_____

_____

_____

_____

_____

_____

_____

_____

_____

_____

_____

_____

_____

_____

_____

_____

_____

_____

_____

► *And you will joyfully give thanks to the Father who has made you able to have a share in all that he has prepared for his people in the kingdom of light.*

COLOSSIANS 1:2 *New Century Version*

▲ ▲ ▲

▼ ▼ ▼

"Faith cannot grow in the atmosphere of condemnation." ◄

— E. W. KENYON

_____

_____

_____

_____

_____

_____

_____

_____

_____

_____

_____

_____

_____

_____

_____

_____

_____

_____

_____

_____

_____

_____

_____

_____

There is therefore now no condemnation to them which are in Christ ◄
Jesus, who walk not after the flesh, but after the Spirit.

ROMANS 8:1

▲ ▲ ▲

▼ ▼ ▼

► *"We don't serve a dead God. We don't serve a God Who has no power. Our God is still God."*

— RODNEY HOWARD-BROWNE

_____

_____

_____

_____

_____

_____

_____

_____

_____

_____

_____

_____

_____

_____

_____

_____

_____

_____

_____

_____

► *Jesus Christ is the same yesterday, today, and forever.*

HEBREWS 13:8 *Simple English Bible*

▲ ▲ ▲

▼ ▼ ▼

"You cannot go by what everything looks like. You have to go by what ◀
God's Word says and trust God. If you cannot trust God, who can you
trust?"

— HAPPY CALDWELL

_____

_____

_____

_____

_____

_____

_____

_____

_____

_____

_____

_____

_____

_____

_____

_____

_____

_____

_____

_____

_____

"Thy word is true from the beginning: and every one of thy righteous ◀
judgments endureth for ever."

PSALM 119:160

▲ ▲ ▲

▼ ▼ ▼

▶ *"A heart full of God has power for the prayer of faith."*

— ANDREW MURRAY

_____

_____

_____

_____

_____

_____

_____

_____

_____

_____

_____

_____

_____

_____

_____

_____

_____

_____

_____

_____

_____

▶ *If you live in Me [abide vitally united to Me] and My words remain in you and continue to live in your hearts, ask whatever you will, and it shall be done for you.*

JOHN 15:7 *Amplified*

▲ ▲ ▲

▼ ▼ ▼

"Men are never nearer heaven, nearer God, never more God-like, never ◄
in deeper sympathy and truer partnership with Jesus Christ, than when
praying."

— E. M. BOUNDS

_____

_____

_____

_____

_____

_____

_____

_____

_____

_____

_____

_____

_____

_____

_____

_____

_____

_____

_____

_____

Thou wilt reveal the path to life, to the full joy of thy presence, to the ◄
bliss of being close to thee for ever.

PSALM 16:11 *Moffatt*

▲ ▲ ▲

▼ ▼ ▼

► *"Prayer must become as natural as breathing. With such prayer, men defeat spiritual forces arrayed against them that no human means could overcome."*

— GORDON LINDSAY

_____

_____

_____

_____

_____

_____

_____

_____

_____

_____

_____

_____

_____

_____

_____

_____

_____

_____

_____

_____

► *Be praying unceasingly.*

1 THESSALONIANS 5:17 *Wuest*

▲ ▲ ▲

▼ ▼ ▼

"Only he who can see the invisible can do the impossible." ◄

— ANONYMOUS

But Jesus beheld them, and said unto them, With men this is impossible; ◄
but with God all things are possible.

MATTHEW 19:26

▲ ▲ ▲

▼ ▼ ▼

► *"While recognizing that the freedom to choose a godly path is the essence of liberty, as a nation we cannot but hope that more of our citizens would, through prayer, come into closer relationship with their Maker."*
— FORMER PRESIDENT RONALD REAGAN

_____

_____

_____

_____

_____

_____

_____

_____

_____

_____

_____

_____

_____

_____

_____

_____

_____

_____

► *Devote yourselves to prayer. Give your whole mind to it, and also offer thanksgiving.*

COLOSSIANS 4:2 *Twentieth Century*

▲ ▲ ▲

▼ ▼ ▼

"Prayer is not to be a religious form with no power. It is to be effective and accurate and bring results!"

— CAROLYN EAST, WORD MINISTRIES

_____

_____

_____

_____

_____

_____

_____

_____

_____

_____

_____

_____

_____

_____

_____

_____

_____

_____

_____

_____

_____

_____

_____

The heartfelt supplication of a righteous man exerts a mighty influence.
JAMES 5:16 *Weymouth*

▲ ▲ ▲

▼ ▼ ▼

► *"A prayer life doesn't mean hours spent in actual prayer, but hours of study and meditation in the Word until the life becomes literally absorbed in the Word and the Word becomes a very part of us."*

— E. W. KENYON

_____

_____

_____

_____

_____

_____

_____

_____

_____

_____

_____

_____

_____

_____

_____

_____

_____

_____

_____

► *This book of the law shall not depart out of thy mouth; but thou shalt meditate therein day and night, that thou mayest observe to do according to all that is written therein: for then thou shalt make thy way prosperous, and then thou shalt have good success.*

JOSHUA 1:8

▲ ▲ ▲

▼ ▼ ▼

"It seems God is limited by our prayer life — that He can do nothing for ◄
humanity unless someone asks Him!"

— JOHN WESLEY

_____

_____

_____

_____

_____

_____

_____

_____

_____

_____

_____

_____

_____

_____

_____

_____

_____

_____

_____

_____

_____

_____

_____

...Ye have not, because of your not asking. ◄
JAMES 4:2 *Young*

▲ ▲ ▲

▼ ▼ ▼

► *"Faith is in the present tense. It believes now. It receives now. It acts now."*

— BILLY JOE DAUGHERTY

_____

_____

_____

_____

_____

_____

_____

_____

_____

_____

_____

_____

_____

_____

_____

_____

_____

_____

_____

_____

_____

► *Now faith is the title deed of things hoped for, the proof of things which are not being seen.*

HEBREWS 11:1 *Wuest*

▲ ▲ ▲

▼ ▼ ▼

"Unless you purposely set your will to accomplish a particular thing, it ◀
will never be done."

— BUDDY HARRISON

_____

_____

_____

_____

_____

_____

_____

_____

_____

_____

_____

_____

_____

_____

_____

_____

_____

_____

_____

_____

_____

_____

...let us run with patient endurance and steady and active persistence ◀
*the appointed course of the race that is set before us, looking away [from
all that will distract] to Jesus, Who is the Leader and the Source of our
faith [giving the first incentive for our belief] and is also its Finisher
[bringing it to maturity and perfection]....*

HEBREWS 12:1,2 *Amplified*

▲ ▲ ▲

▼ ▼ ▼

► *"All it takes to receive from God is a little bit of faith in a great big God."*

— KENNETH HAGIN, JR.

_____

_____

_____

_____

_____

_____

_____

_____

_____

_____

_____

_____

_____

_____

_____

_____

_____

_____

_____

_____

_____

► *And Jesus said unto them, Because of your unbelief: for verily I say unto you, If ye have faith as a grain of mustard seed, ye shall say unto this mountain, Remove hence to yonder place; and it shall remove; and nothing shall be impossible unto you.*

MATTHEW 17:20

▲ ▲ ▲

▼ ▼ ▼

"Faith must rest on the will of God alone, not on our desires or wishes." ◄

— F. F. BOSWORTH

_____

_____

_____

_____

_____

_____

_____

_____

_____

_____

_____

_____

_____

_____

_____

_____

_____

_____

_____

_____

_____

_____

And this is the confidence we have resting on Him, that if we petition ◄
anything in agreement with His will, He hears us.

1 JOHN 5:14 *Berkeley*

▲ ▲ ▲

▼ ▼ ▼

► *"He that dwelleth in the secret place of the Most High need fear no evil. God will send His angels to protect the man or woman who prays."*

— GORDON LINDSAY

_____

_____

_____

_____

_____

_____

_____

_____

_____

_____

_____

_____

_____

_____

_____

_____

_____

_____

_____

_____

_____

► *He that dwelleth in the secret place of the most High shall abide under the shadow of the Almighty. Because thou hast made the Lord, which is my refuge, even the most High, thy habitation; there shall no evil befall thee, neither shall any plague come nigh thy dwelling. For he shall give his angels charge over thee, to keep thee in all thy ways.*

PSALM 91:1, 9 - 11

▲ ▲ ▲

▼ ▼ ▼

► *"Let our one desire be to take time and be still before God, believing with an unbounded faith in His longing to make Himself known to us."*
— ANDREW MURRAY

_____

_____

_____

_____

_____

_____

_____

_____

_____

_____

_____

_____

_____

_____

_____

_____

_____

_____

_____

_____

_____

_____

_____

► *Be still, and know that I am God: I will be exalted among the heathen, I will be exalted in the earth.*
PSALM 46:10

▲ ▲ ▲

▼ ▼ ▼

"The deepest working of the Holy Spirit comes during the time spent ◄
alone in His presence."

— DENNIS BURKE

_____

_____

_____

_____

_____

_____

_____

_____

_____

_____

_____

_____

_____

_____

_____

_____

_____

_____

_____

_____

_____

_____

But he would always go off to some place where he could be alone and ◄
pray.

LUKE 5:16 *Jerusalem*

▲ ▲ ▲

▼ ▼ ▼

"If you expect the Lord to do wonderful things for you, He will." ◄

— ORAL ROBERTS

_____

_____

_____

_____

_____

_____

_____

_____

_____

_____

_____

_____

_____

_____

_____

_____

_____

_____

_____

_____

_____

_____

And delight thyself on Jehovah, and He giveth to thee the petitions of ◄
thy heart.

PSALM 73:4 *Young*

▲ ▲ ▲

▼ ▼ ▼

► *"Like Christ, we gain our strength to stand and not faint through prayer and communion with God."*

— ORAL ROBERTS

_____

_____

_____

_____

_____

_____

_____

_____

_____

_____

_____

_____

_____

_____

_____

_____

_____

_____

_____

_____

► *But you, my dear friends, must keep building yourselves up in your most holy faith. You must pray in the Holy Spirit.*

JUDE 20 *Laubach*

▲ ▲ ▲

▼ ▼ ▼

"Do become one of those intercessors who really believe that in answer ◄
to your prayer Jesus will do far more than you can ask or think."
— ANDREW MURRAY

_____

_____

_____

_____

_____

_____

_____

_____

_____

_____

_____

_____

_____

_____

_____

_____

_____

_____

_____

_____

_____

_____

_____

To him who by means of his power working in us is able to do so much ◄
more than we can ever ask for, or even think of.
EPHESIANS 3:20 *Good News*

▲ ▲ ▲

▼ ▼ ▼

► *"Faith works by love. Love gives and forgives. So faith can't operate without love."*

— BUDDY HARRISON

_____

_____

_____

_____

_____

_____

_____

_____

_____

_____

_____

_____

_____

_____

_____

_____

_____

_____

_____

_____

► *For [if we are] in Christ Jesus, neither circumcision nor uncircumcision counts for anything, but only faith activated and energized and expressed and working through love.*

GALATIANS 5:6 *Amplified*

▲ ▲ ▲

▼ ▼ ▼

"We come to God through faith — all other manifestations of the ◄
majesty and glory of God come the same way."

— LESTER SUMRALL

_____

_____

_____

_____

_____

_____

_____

_____

_____

_____

_____

_____

_____

_____

_____

_____

_____

_____

_____

_____

_____

Therefore I say to you, all things for which you pray and ask, believe ◄
that you have received them, and they shall be granted you.

MARK 11:24 *New American Standard*

▲ ▲ ▲

▼ ▼ ▼

► *"Fellowship in its fullness is the soil out of which living faith grows to fruition."*

— E. W. KENYON

_____

_____

_____

_____

_____

_____

_____

_____

_____

_____

_____

_____

_____

_____

_____

_____

_____

_____

_____

_____

► *Maintain a living communion with me, and I with you. Just as the branch is unable to be bearing fruit from itself as a source unless it remains in a living union with the vine, so neither you, unless you maintain a living communion with me.*

JOHN 15:4 *Wuest*

▲ ▲ ▲

▼ ▼ ▼

"Be quick to repent and quick to forgive and you'll never be far from ◄
God."

— KENNETH E. HAGIN

_____

_____

_____

_____

_____

_____

_____

_____

_____

_____

_____

_____

_____

_____

_____

_____

_____

_____

_____

_____

_____

And when ye stand praying, forgive if ye have anything against any- ◄
one, that your Father also who is in the heavens may forgive you your
offences.

MARK 11:25 *Darby*

▲ ▲ ▲

Bibles Quoted

Amplified. *The Amplified Bible, Old Testament,* Grand Rapids: Zondervan, 1965, 1987. *New Testament,* La Habra, California: The Lockman Foundation, 1958, 1987.

Basic English. *The Bible in Basic English.* New York: Cambridge University Press, 1949, 1965.

Berkeley. *The Holy Bible: The Berkeley Version in Modern English,* Gerrit Verkuyl, Ph.D., Editor-In-Chief and Translator of New Testament Section. Grand Rapids, Zondervan, 1945, 1958.

Concordant Literal. *The Sacred Scriptures Concordant Literal New Testament with Key Word Concordance.* Canyon Country, California: Concordant Publishing Concern, 1983.

Darby. *The Holy Scriptures, A New Translation from the Original Languages.* J. N. Darby. Sussex, England: A. J. Holman Company, 1975.

Fenton. *The Holy Bible in Modern English.* Ferrar Fenton M.R.A.S., M.C.A.A. Merrimac, Massachusetts: Destiny Publishers, n.d.

Good News. *Good News Bible, The Bible in Today's English Version.* New York: American Bible Society, 1966, 1971, 1976.

Jerusalem. *The Jerusalem Bible.* Garden City, New York: Doubleday and Company, 1966.

Laubach. *The Inspired Letters in Clearest English.* Frank C. Laubach, Ph.D. New York: Thomas Nelson and Sons, 1956.

Living Oracles. *The Living Oracles, The New Testament.* Alexander Campbell, n.p., n.d.

Moffatt. *A New Translation of the Bible.* James Moffatt. London: Hodder and Stoughton Limited, 1926.

New Century Version. *The Holy Bible, New Century Version.* Dallas, Texas 75039: Word Publishing, 1987, 1988, 1991.

New American Standard Bible. *New American Standard Bible.* La Habra, California: The Lockman Foundation, 1960, 1962, 1963, 1968, 1971, 1972, 1973, 1975, 1977.

New International Version. *Holy Bible, New International Version®.* NIV®. Grand Rapids: Zondervan. Copyright © 1973, 1978, 1984 by International Bible Society.

New King James Version. *The New King James Version* of the Bible. Nashville: Thomas Nelson, 1979, 1980, 1982.

New Life Version. *Holy Bible, New Life Version.* Gleason Ledyard. Canby, Oregon. Copyright © 1969, 1976, 1978, 1983, 1986 by Christian Literature International.

Simple English Bible. *The Simple English Bible,* American Edition. New York: International Bible Publishing Company, 1981.

Twentieth Century. *The Twentieth Century New Testament, A Translation into Modern English,* A Tentative Edition. Chicago: Fleming H. Revell, 1898, 1900, 1901.

Weymouth. *The New Testament in Modern Speech.* Richard Francis Weymouth M.A., D.Lit. Edited and partly revised by Ernest Hampden-Cook, M.A., 3d ed. London: James Clarke and Company, 1909.

Worrell. *The Worrell New Testament.* Copyright © 1904 by A. S. Worrell assigned to the Assemblies of God. Springfield, Missouri 65802: Gospel Publishing House, 1980.

Wuest. *The New Testament, An Expanded Translation.* Kenneth S. Wuest. Grand Rapids: Wm. B. Eerdmans Publishing Company, 1956, 1958, 1959, 1961.

Young. *Young's Literal Translation of the Holy Bible.* Robert Young. Rev. ed. Grand Rapids: Baker Book House, n.d.

ANSWERED PRAYER

ANSWERED PRAYER

ANSWERED PRAYER

SALVATION
REGISTER
FAMILY & FRIENDS

Believe in the Lord Jesus Christ...and you will be saved...you and your household as well.

ACTS 16:31 *Amplified*

Name	Date	Name	Date